Sinners
A

A few years back while visiting a popular church in a Chicago suburb, I heard "a good, old-fashioned hellfire-and-brimstone sermon," as they used to call it. Few listeners in the large congregation fell asleep.

The speaker grabbed everyone's attention with his vivid description of sinners sizzling and screaming in hellfire. After considerable emphasis on the horrors of hell, the speaker shifted to a discussion of how long eternity is. His colorful illustrations and down-to-earth presentation soon convinced his listeners that human beings cannot possibly comprehend eternity.

Suddenly he directed his audience to the terrors of a hell that burns on endlessly, eternally, forever. No death releases the sinner from hell. Unconsciousness cannot free him. He or she has nowhere to turn, hopelessly trapped by the wrath of a vengeful God who metes out eternal punishment to every man, woman, and child who has not been born again and baptized.

Needless to say, the altar call that morning brought forty-seven souls to the front of the auditorium—twenty-eight of whom the speaker baptized *that very morning*.

During the baptism I couldn't help asking myself how many of those twenty-eight persons "buried in the waters of salvation" were seeking a day-by-day living experience with the Saviour rather than a quick ticket out of the flames of eternal hell.

No wonder, I reminded myself, so many people become atheists: How could anyone love a God who could condone and conduct that kind of horrendous activity? And carry it on forever? Unceasing? Throughout all eternity? Is that really what the Bible teaches? Is that the loving God who gave His Son so we may live?

The Inconsistency of an Eternally Burning Hell

Assuming for the moment that God plans to punish the wicked for their sins, why do it eternally? Wouldn't, say, 10,000 years suffice? Or perhaps 70,000 years—a thousand years of punishment for each year of an average life on earth? Why eternally, with no end?

What would be the *purpose* of endless fiery torture? Let's list a few possibilities:

1. A punishment for sins committed
2. A deterrent against present sinning
3. A deterrent against future sin
4. The reformation of the sinner
5. The purification of the sinner
6. Appeasement for a vindictive God

Now, let's examine these possible reasons for an eternally burning hell.

1. A punishment for sins committed? Even earthly judges realize that punishment should not exceed the offense. Long ago the human race pulled itself out of the irrationality of the Dark Ages, when, some historians say, a man or woman could lose a hand or head for stealing a loaf of bread.

Earthly parents also recognize that one does not spend five hours spanking a child who has colored the wall with crayon, even if that child has been warned

4

repeatedly not to mark on the walls. A spanking that lasts longer than necessary only develops a spirit of hatred and rebellion in the child's heart. Can you imagine the hatred that would be fueled by ten billion sinners burning throughout all eternity? How could eternal justice support such an act?

Abraham declared, "Shall not the Judge of all the earth do right?" (Genesis 18:25). Even Jesus Himself, who is our Judge (see John 5:22), said, "I judge: and my judgment is just" (John 5:30). Certainly we can trust God to judge justly and to deal with sinners appropriately, but punishing them eternally defies all standards of justice and even common sense.

2. A deterrent against present sinning? Experts who have conducted extensive studies of America's penal code, and especially of states which have death penalties, claim the death penalty is not a deterrent against crime. Criminals, they say, commit as many crimes, even as many violent ones, in states with death penalties as in states without the death penalty.

The question posed by the prophet Jeremiah applies: "Can the Ethiopian change his skin, or the leopard his spots? then may ye also do good, that are accustomed to do evil" (Jeremiah 13:23). Goodness comes only from a transformation of heart caused by an indwelling of Christ through the Holy Spirit. Certainly the sinner cannot change his own heart, nor will the change happen as a result of some threatened period of punishment. The purpose of the lake of fire—as we shall soon see—is to destroy, not to punish.

3. A deterrent against future sin? To whom would this deterrent apply? To the righteous who have already been redeemed—those already experiencing the joys and delights of the universe? Certainly not!

To the wicked? No. If anything, their sinful, vengeful attitudes while sizzling in the lake of eternal fire would increase, not decrease. The excessive punishment would serve to perpetuate sin, not eradicate it, thus guaranteeing that God's universe would be constantly tainted by sin. We would end up with a universe full of eternal hate and rebellion.

4. *A reformation for the sinner?* Does anyone really believe that an eternally burning hell could truly reform a sinner? No person tormented year after year in a lake of fire and facing nothing but the same forever could experience true conversion. People would say anything, profess anything, promise anything, just to obtain release. Like Judas, they would admit their sin (see Matthew 27:4), but their repentance would be just as false as was his.

5. *A purification of the sinner?* Iron and gold can be purified by fire. So can lead, copper, and silver. But fire cannot purify flesh and bone, nor can it cleanse souls.

Years ago, prior to the Reformation, the Roman church taught that indulgences paid or performed by relatives of the dead would release their loved ones prior to the expected termination of their sentence in purgatory. A famous phrase uttered by Johann Tetzel, a sixteenth-century German Dominican preacher, was this:

> As soon as the coin in the coffer rings,
> The soul from purgatory springs.

This jingle did much to evoke the response of Martin Luther, thus launching the Protestant Reformation.

Of all the arguments we have discussed in this section, this one has no doubt been promoted the most. Both Dante's *Inferno* and John Bunyan's *Pilgrim's Progress* depict the purifying, cleansing powers of hell. Fortunately, few Christians today accept this explanation for an eternally burning hell.

6. An appeasement for a vengeful God? While it is true that the Bible, especially in the Old Testament, speaks of God's vengeance upon the wicked, nowhere is this vengeance considered eternal. Such a thought is completely foreign to God's Word.

Rather, references to God's vengeance should more properly be viewed as to *avenge*, rather than to *revenge.* Revenge is a sinful human emotion foreign to the compassion and loving nature of the King of the universe. Unger's *Bible Dictionary* says, "When vengeance is predicted of the Lord it must be taken in the better sense of righteous punishment."

Certainly, God's character and position in the conflict of the ages needs vindication during the day of judgment. But that vindication does not require sinners to be punished with eternal fire and torments that never cease. Nothing about eternal torment would help vindicate God's character. On the contrary, His judgment would be subject to question throughout all eternity. Eternal suffering would constantly reopen the wound every time one of the redeemed thought of his or her parent or spouse or son or daughter suffering in the lake of hellfire.

Before concluding this section on the inconsistencies of an eternally burning hell, we must consider one other major problem created by the popular belief that when one dies he goes directly to heaven or hell. If this belief is true (and it is taught by perhaps 90 percent of all ministers and theologians), what about the day of judgment?

John the revelator describes that day with these words:

I saw a great white throne, and him that sat

on it, from whose face the earth and the heaven fled away; and there was found no place for them. And I saw the dead, small and great, stand before God; and the books were opened: and another book was opened, which is the book of life: and the dead were judged out of those things which were written in the books, according to their works. . . . And whosoever was not found written in the book of life was cast into the lake of fire (Revelation 20:11-15).

Can you imagine the difficulty of believing on one hand that rewards are passed out as soon as one dies and, on the other, that one's destiny is decided on the great day of judgment, which is yet future? The wicked in hell would have to come out, be judged, and then be cast back in!

Why have a "day of judgment" (2 Peter 2:9) in which humans receive their rewards if they already have their reward when they die?

Why does the Bible declare that God will destroy the wicked on the "day of judgment and perdition of ungodly men" (2 Peter 3:7)? It doesn't say He will punish them both before and after the day of judgment, but at the day of judgment.

As we can see, the six reasons set forth by those who believe that God punishes sinners throughout eternity lack biblical or even common-sense credibility. We have also discussed the incongruity of a sinner receiving his sentence of damnation when he dies, only to be resurrected and to be sentenced again in the day of judgment. With so many inconsistencies, why do so many people and even theologians believe in the popular teaching regarding eternal hellfire?

How the Popular Belief Developed

Although we haven't yet discussed what the Bible itself teaches (and doesn't teach) about hell, no doubt the reader by now wonders how the popular belief in an eternally burning hell developed.

If an eternally burning hell is not a deterrent for present or future sin, if it's not an object lesson for other worlds, if it's not for the reformation or purification of sinners, and if it's not to appease a vindictive God—why, then, do so many churches still believe in everlasting hellfire? To answer this question we'll have to check our history books.

The concept of an abode of the dead, although taking many different forms, occurs in the folklore and mythology of many lands and peoples throughout history. Over the years people have viewed the dwelling place of the dead as (1) a gloomy subterranean realm or some distant island no man-made ship could reach (Greek *Hades*); (2) an underworld of cold and darkness (Norse *Nifleimr*, called *Hel*); (3) a deep abyss where souls are punished (Greek *Tartarus*); (4) the tomb in which the body was placed (in Egypt, called the "house of eternity"); (5) a celestial dwelling place where the departed reside (Pueblo Indians believed the departed became clouds); and (6) a nebulous existence in which the soul eventually fades into nonexistence (North American Indian hunting tribes).

Judaism, as reflected in the Old Testament (*i.e.*, prior to the second century B.C.), possessed an uncomplicated understanding about life after death. In every occurrence of *sheol* (translated "grave" or "hell") in the Old Testament (sixty-five times), the word means nothing more than the place where the dead sleep (see Job 17:13; Psalm 31:17; Isaiah 38:18). Nowhere in the Old Testament will one find a teaching akin to the beliefs of other ancient cultures regarding the place or status of the dead.

However, during the period between the Old and New Testaments the Jews came into close contact with the Persians and the Greeks, both of whom possessed well-developed ideas about the world of the dead.

The religion of the Persian Empire, Zoroastrianism, taught that the soul, after waiting three days for judgment then had to cross the Bridge of the Requiter. If the person committed many evil deeds during his life, the bridge became impassable and he fell into an ill-smelling, freezing hell, there to suffer torment. The Greek Orphic sects, on the other hand, taught the immortality of the soul—a concept developed in considerable detail by Plato.

By the time of Christ the Jews generally had adopted both of these teachings—that the wicked soul would be punished after death for varying lengths of time (but never exceeding twelve months except for heresy) and that the soul is immortal.

However, we should point out that these beliefs came from the Persians and Greeks and not by revelation of God through the Old Testament prophets. In fact, Jesus Himself tried to correct His disciples' beliefs about the condition of the dead when He claimed death was nothing more than a person's sleeping in the grave (see John 11:11-14). It is obvious from the disciples' reaction to His description (verse 13) that this teaching conflicted with their own Jewish training.

With this background, let's look at the use of *hell* in both the Old and New Testaments. The English word *hell* comes from an Anglo-Saxon verb meaning "to conceal," "to cover." It originally meant "the concealed, hidden, or covered place."

Old English literature speaks of the *helling* of a

house—meaning to roof it or thatch it, and of the *helling* of potatoes—placing potatoes into ditches and covering them with dirt. Several hundred years ago the word *hell*, as then understood, could properly translate the Hebrew *sheol* and Greek *hades*, which referred to the abode of the dead.

Let's now look at the four Hebrew and Greek words that were translated "hell" in the King James Bible.

1. Sheol. The Hebrew *sheol*, which occurs sixty-five times in the Old Testament, appears (KJV) as "grave" thirty-one times, "hell" thirty-one times, and "pit" three times. If one consults a concordance to the KJV Bible, he will quickly discover that in every one of the thirty-one instances when the Hebrew *sheol* is translated "hell," it could as easily have been translated "the grave."

One example will illustrate the point: Amos 9:2—"Though they dig into hell [*sheol*], thence shall mine hand take them." Can humans dig into hell? Of course not. But people can dig into the grave.

2. Hades. Hades, the Greek equivalent of *sheol,* occurs eleven times in the New Testament. Although the KJV translates this word as "hell" ten times, more modern versions indicate that this was unwarranted. In fact, the New International Version (NIV) uses "depths," "grave," and "death" for five of those occurrences. In the five remaining instances, the NIV simply gives the Greek word in English letters (*i.e.,* "hades") without attempting to identify the meaning.

However, one can see from Revelation 20:14 and Acts 2:27 that to translate the Greek *hades* as either "hell" or "hades" leads to confusion. That is, Can hell be cast *into* a lake of fire? Did Jesus go to *hell* when He died? Significantly, in Asia Minor the word *hades* appears on many ancient tombstones, indicating the grave of a particular person.

3. *Gehenna.* Twelve times in the New Testament the word "hell" is a translation of the *gehenna,* the Greek transliteration of *ge Hinnom,* the Hebrew for "the valley of Hinnom"—a 200- to 300-foot-deep garbage dump just outside the west and south walls of ancient Jerusalem.

This valley, in addition to its use as a place for burning garbage and refuse, held a much deeper significance for the Jews of Christ's time. Although only the worst criminals received a sentence of death, the Sanhedrin—the seventy-one-member high court which supervised the gravest offenses—could subject very obnoxious criminals to the double indignity of being refused burial and being cast along with the carcasses of dogs in the city dump (*i.e.,* into the Valley of Hinnom, or *gehenna*), there to be consumed by the garbage-dump fires.

The purpose of this burning in *gehenna* was to make the criminal and his crimes utterly detestable in the people's eyes and to indicate that the culprit was eternally lost because of his deeds. (Remember that the Jews generally, other than the Sadducees, anticipated a resurrection from the tomb and therefore took particular care regarding the corpses of the dead.)

Hence, the condemnation of the corpse to *gehenna,* which destroyed it, signified, as the Jew saw it, the loss of any future life through resurrection. *Gehenna* to the Jew of Christ's time symbolized the second death (see Revelation 20:14, 15) as no other illustration possibly could.

With this in mind, we can easily understand Christ's frequent reference to the Valley of Hinnom as an apt description of the condition of the lost—rejected by their own people, cast aside with the dogs and garbage, utterly destroyed in the refuse fires, and with no hope of a second probation. No resident of Jerusalem in Christ's time could have applied *gehenna* to a place of eternal torment.

Therefore, if the New Testament reader will simply substitute the Greek word *gehenna*, or "garbage dump," in each of the following passages—Matthew 5:22, 29, 30; 10:28; 18:9; 23:15, 33; Mark 9:43-47; Luke 12:5; James 3:6—where "hell" appears in the King James Version, he will have no difficulty understanding Christ's meaning and intent.

4. Tartaroo. In 2 Peter 2:4 only does this word appear in the Greek Bible. *Tartaroo* is a Greek term that referred to the abode of the wicked dead. Peter, writing to Christians in a Hellenistic culture, employs a Greek term apparently in symbolism. Peter's reference to "chains of darkness," for example, indicates his figurative description of that place where evil angels are being held in a state of condemnation until the day of God's judgment. Nothing in this passage supports the popular concept that these evil angels, or demons, carry out any punishment against lost sinners or that they torture anyone. In fact, nothing in this passage even hints about hellfire flames in this place or state.

The Rich Man and Lazarus Story

Some believe that the story of the rich man and Lazarus teaches hell does exist. We find the narrative recorded in Luke 16:19-31:

> There was a certain rich man, which was clothed in purple and fine linen, and fared sumptuously every day: and there was a certain beggar named Lazarus, which was laid at his gate full of sores, and desiring to be fed with the crumbs which fell from the rich

13

man's table. . . . And it came to pass, that the beggar died, and was carried by the angels into Abraham's bosom: the rich man also died, and was buried; and in hell he lift up his eyes, being in torments, and seeth Abraham afar off, and Lazarus in his bosom. And he cried and said, Father Abraham, have mercy on me, and send Lazarus, that he may dip the tip of his finger in water, and cool my tongue; for I am tormented in this flame. But Abraham said, Son, remember that thou in thy lifetime receivedst thy good things, and likewise Lazarus evil things: but now he is comforted, and thou art tormented. And beside all this, between us and you there is a great gulf fixed: so that they which would pass from hence to you cannot; neither can they pass to us, that would come from thence. Then he said, I pray thee therefore, father, that thou wouldest send him to my father's house: for I have five brethren; that he may testify unto them, lest they also come into this place of torment. Abraham saith unto him, They have Moses and the prophets; let them hear them. And he said, Nay, father Abraham: but if one went unto them from the dead, they will repent. And he said unto him, If they hear not Moses and the prophets, neither will they be persuaded, though one rose from the dead.

Should we accept this account as a literal description of hell or as a parable which teaches a specific lesson perhaps unrelated to the details of the story? If we view it as a literal description of hell, as many Christians do, a formidable array of problems immediately confronts us:

14

1. If a literal description, then Christ teaches that poor people go to heaven and rich people to hell (verses 22, 23). This obviously contradicts John 3:16 ("that *whosoever* believeth in him should not perish, but have everlasting life").

2. In hell the spirits apparently have literal fingers, eyes, tongues, and mouths—complete with nerves which can feel pain, thirst, etc. (Luke 16:23, 24). This, however, conflicts with the popular teaching today about how a soul or spirit is composed after death.

3. People in paradise, also, apparently can communicate with people in hell, and vice versa (verses 24-31). And people in hell can plead with those in heaven, pray for relief, and beg for help (verses 24, 27).

4. People in heaven can see the residents of hell as they are tormented (verse 25).

5. Abraham, in some way, is the spokesman for the righteous in heaven (verse 24).

6. Heaven is actually "Abraham's bosom" (verse 22) and not a place in some other location in the universe.

Obviously, even the staunchest proponents of the rich man and Lazarus account would reject the application of the details above. How could all the righteous live in Abraham's bosom? How can spirits have flesh, bone, and nerves? Why should rich men go to hell and poor men to heaven? How could heaven ever be a heaven if the saved could witness over a chasm the suffering of the wicked? In fact, how could anyone—any parent with a child in hell, a wife with a husband in hell, a child with its mother in hell, or a brother with his sister in hell—ever enjoy heaven, knowing that his dear relative is burning in hellfire throughout all eternity?

However, if those in hell can beg and plead with

those in heaven for relief and assistance, what kind of hell would that make heaven? What kind of God could invent such a horrible future—for the lost or the saved? Heaven would become more a hell than hell itself.

Certainly no one can accept the details of this account as facts about the future life. It is obviously a parable, not a true story. Even the famous theologian A. H. Strong admits, "We grant that the material images used in Scripture to set forth the sufferings of the lost are to be spiritually and not literally interpreted."—*Systematic Theology*, p. 1056. This confession from a believer in everlasting hellfire should carry considerable weight in any discussion of this parable.

Now, if we reject the details regarding Abraham's bosom, flesh-and-bone spirits, a gulf over which the wicked and righteous can see and talk, and Abraham as the guardian of the righteous and wicked—why should we cling to any other detail used in this story? Like the eternal torment of the wicked?

One shouldn't reject six items as fictional or symbolic and then claim the seventh as literal. That's inconsistent. How much better to accept the story for what it is and nothing more: a parable intended to teach a basic lesson, but not necessarily conveying incidental truths in addition.

One primary rule that applies to every parable in the Bible is that a parable contains one main lesson or teaching. The parable must not be forced into a corner and pressured to make additional comments unrelated to that teaching. Consequently, we must always beware of reaching unwarranted conclusions from incidental events or details in a parable that have no real bearing on the lesson being taught. These fundamental principles of biblical interpretation naturally apply to the parable of the rich man and Lazarus.

But, some may counter, *doesn't the parable indicate that the dead are alive and can communicate with each other?* In a way, yes. But unless the actors are given the opportunity to speak, how else can the story be told? Let's look at another parable in the Scriptures for a good illustration of this technique:

> The trees went forth on a time to anoint a king over them; and they said unto the olive tree, Reign thou over us. But the olive tree said unto them, Should I leave my fatness . . . and go to be promoted over the trees? And the trees said to the fig tree, Come thou, and reign over us. But the fig tree said unto them, Should I forsake my sweetness, and my good fruit, and go to be promoted over the trees? Then said the trees unto the vine, Come thou, and reign over us. And the vine said unto them, Should I leave my wine, which cheereth God and man, and go to be promoted over the trees? Then said all the trees unto the bramble, Come thou, and reign over us. And the bramble said unto the trees, If in truth ye anoint me king over you, then come and put your trust in my shadow (Judges 9:8-15).

Since this story appears in the Bible, should we conclude that trees speak to each other and move themselves about in the ground? Of course not! That takes the parable further than it is intended to go. Trees can no more talk than can the righteous fit into Abraham's bosom or the suffering wicked be seen from the heavenly side of the chasm.

Obviously, in the parable of the rich man and Lazarus Christ intended to state the simple truth that men and women determine their eternal destiny in this life before they die. No one has a second chance after death. The choice must be made now, today. This is the sole intent of the story. We dare not push the account beyond this single lesson.

A quick check of the context—the circumstances which prompted Jesus to relate it—reveals that He was specifically addressing the Pharisees (see Luke 16:14). Jesus answered their mockery with the statement, "God knoweth your hearts: for [he] . . . which is highly esteemed among men is abomination in the sight of God" (verse 15). Shortly thereafter He began relating the story of "a certain rich man, which was clothed in purple and fine linen" (verse 19).

Significantly, in speaking to the Pharisees, Jesus employed in this parable a number of details already accepted as fact by the Pharisees. Let us compare Christ's parable with statements about Hades recorded in Josephus's book *Discourse to the Greeks Concerning Hades* (which was written shortly after Christ's crucifixion, thus reflecting Jewish thinking of the first century A.D.).

Christ's Parable	Josephus's Book
"a certain rich man . . . *fared sumptuously.*"	"whomsoever shall have lived wickedly and *luxuriously.*"
"the beggar . . . was *carried by the angels*"	"are led . . . *by the angels*"
"the beggar . . . was carried . . . into *Abraham's bosom*"	"in . . . the *Bosom of Abraham.*"

18

"I am *tormented* in this flame"	"an exceeding great . . . fire even *hereby are they punished*"
"between us and you there is *a great gulf fixed*"	"for a *chaos deep and large is fixed* between them"

Christ's account obviously comes from the Jewish beliefs of His day. Jesus employed a parable which the Pharisees, to whom He was speaking, would readily recognize. He used their language to thrust home an important point, much as a Christian missionary might use a passage from the Koran to convince a Muslim in Pakistan or one from the *Doctrine of the Mean* for a follower of Confucious in China.

But His use of material familiar to the Pharisees should not cause us to draw the erroneous conclusion that He supported their beliefs about the future state of human beings. The parable differs too much from the teaching of the rest of Scripture.

In this analysis of the parable of the rich man and Lazarus we have learned three important lessons: (1) the details of a parable carry no significance on their own, except as "props" for the main lesson; (2) making the details of this parable teach specific doctrine in addition to the parable's main lesson leads to at least seven major errors about the future state; (3) a parable couched in terms familiar to a group specifically addressed should not be interpreted to be the beliefs of the speaker.

The claim that Jesus intended this parable to teach that both the good and the wicked receive their rewards at death violates all three of these rules. It also contradicts Christ's own declaration that "the

Son of man shall come in the glory of his Father with his angels; and then he shall reward every man according to his works" (Matthew 16:27. See also Matthew 25:31-41; 1 Corinthians 15:51-55; 1 Thessalonians 4:16, 17; Revelation 22:12). Therefore, it seems wise to discount this parable *as a medium of teaching truth about hell.*

Eternally Burning Fire?

A while back I received a free ticket in the mail (bearing the foreboding number 666) which entitled the holder "to spend eternity in the lake of fire with the devil and his angels." The price of admission? According to the ticket: "to do nothing and ignore God's saving grace."

Fortunately the publisher of this ticket for eternity included another ticket on the reverse side which entitled the bearer "to spend eternity in heaven with Jesus Christ the Son of God."

While we may find such a novelty humorous, it unfortunately cancels the good it could accomplish by echoing the familiar but unbiblical teaching that hellfire burns forever, unceasingly, throughout eternity. Does the Bible support the existence of such a fire—one that burns eternally?

Most people who hold such a belief base their ideas on the two occasions when Jesus employed the expression "everlasting fire" (see Matthew 18:8; 25:41). Let's examine this expression to discover what it really teaches: "Then shall he say also unto them on the left hand, Depart from me, ye cursed, into everlasting fire, prepared for the devil and his angels" (Matthew 25:41).

Obviously, the hellfire can't go out in one place (see Malachi 4:1, 3) and burn eternally in another. Could Jesus have been talking about the *kind* of fire that destroys the wicked, rather than the *duration* of that fire?

In both Matthew 25:41 and Matthew 18:8 the Greek word that appears in the original text is *aionios*—which in Mark 3:29 (KJV) is translated "eternal damnation"; in Hebrews 6:2 (KJV), "eternal judgment"; and in Jude 7 (KJV), "eternal fire." Does the use of *aionios* in these passages refer to activity or effect?

Take Hebrews 6:2, for example: "Of the doctrine of baptisms, and of laying on of hands, and of resurrection of the dead, and of eternal judgment." Does this passage mean that the process of judgment continues throughout all eternity? Of course not! Scriptures elsewhere clearly identify judgment as "the day of judgment" (see Matthew 10:15; 12:36; Mark 6:11; 2 Peter 2:9; 3:7; 1 John 4:17).

Obviously *aionios* in Hebrews 6:2 identifies the *kind* of judgment, not its *length,* or *duration.* And so likewise *aionios* refers to the kind of fire that destroys the wicked. Hellfire is eternal in its nature, not in its duration. God's fire which destroys the wicked is an *act* of destruction whose *results* are eternal, not a *process* that goes on forever.

Can we verify from the Scriptures that *aionios* means kind rather than duration when used with the word *fire?* Yes. Look at Jude 7, where the identical Greek phrase is found that occurs in Matthew 18:8 and 25:41: "Even as Sodom and Gomorrah, and the cities about them in like manner, giving themselves over to fornication, and going after strange flesh, are set forth for an example, suffering the vengeance of eternal fire."

The cities of Sodom and Gomorrah perished many centuries before Jude wrote his letter (see Genesis 19:23-28). They were reduced to ashes: "Turning the cities of Sodom and Gomorrah into ashes . . . , making

21

them an ensample unto those that after should live ungodly" (2 Peter 2:6).

Just as the "eternal fire" of Sodom and Gomorrah burned out when it completed its work of destruction, so will the "eternal fire" that destroys the wicked burn out when it devours the wicked (see Hebrews 10:26, 27). God's eternal fire is not eternal in its duration, but in its results. Its *effects* will be everlasting—a complete, total, and permanent destruction! "They shall consume; into smoke shall they consume away" (Psalm 37:20).

One other phrase used by those who believe in an eternally burning hell is "for ever and ever." It occurs twice—both in the book of Revelation.

Biblical scholars know that this phrase, "and her [their] smoke rose up for ever and ever," is derived from Isaiah 34:10. Although some claim that these passages in Isaiah and Revelation teach that the smoke of hell ascends into the universe forever, a quick check of the context in Isaiah 34 disproves this contention.

Referring to the city of Bozrah, an Edomite town about twenty miles southeast of the Dead Sea (see verse 6), Isaiah declared:

> The land thereof shall become burning pitch.
> It [the fire] shall not be quenched night nor
> day; the smoke thereof shall go up for ever:
> from generation to generation it shall lie
> waste; . . . the cormorant [pelican] and the bit-
> tern shall possess it. . . . And thorns shall
> come up in her palaces, nettles and brambles
> in the fortresses thereof (verses 9-13).

From its primary source in Isaiah we discover that the fire which destroys, causing smoke to ascend "for ever and ever," *does not burn forever*. To the Hebrew mind that expression meant complete destruction, not endless burning. Else how could thorns, nettles, and brambles grow up and wild animals take possession?

Jeremiah, talking about the same city, said, "I have sworn by myself, saith the Lord, that Bozrah *shall become a desolation,* a reproach, a waste, and a curse; and all the cities thereof *shall be perpetual wastes*" (Jeremiah 49:13). This is the destiny of the wicked. They will be completely burned up. They will die in this "eternal fire"; the *effect* will last throughout all eternity—a permanent, complete annihilation.

Eight Reasons to Reject Eternal Torment

Many Christians have been taught that the wicked at death pass into hellfire, there to suffer endless torture by a vengeful God. We have already discussed the key scriptural passages that have led sincere theologians and other Christians into such a position: the parable of the rich man and Lazarus; and the expressions "everlasting fire (unquenchable fire)" and "eternal fire," both of which discuss the kind of fire that burns the wicked, not how long it burns.

Further, we have supplied Bible proof that these and similar expressions did not teach that hellfire burns forever. For example, Sodom and Gomorrah are "set forth for an example, suffering the vengeance of eternal fire" (Jude 7), yet having in reality been reduced to ashes (see 2 Peter 2:6). Here now in a condensed form are eight reasons why Christians who study the Scriptures should reject such a doctrine as unbiblical.

1. We reject the teaching of eternal torment because it claims the lost will live forever, which is contrary to Scripture's plainest testimony. "The soul that sinneth, it shall die" (Ezekiel 18:20). "He that hath the Son hath life; and he that hath not the Son of God hath not life" (1 John 5:12). "He which converteth the sinner from the error of his way, shall save a soul from death" (James 5:20). "No murderer hath eternal life abiding in him" (1 John 3:15).

2. *We reject the teaching of eternal torment because it misrepresents our God of love, substituting a being whose wrath is never appeased.* God is "not willing that any should perish, but that all should come to repentance" (2 Peter 3:9).

3. *We reject the teaching of eternal torment because it cannot be reconciled with the picture the Bible gives of Christ.* Jesus said, "Suffer [permit] little children, and forbid them not, to come unto me: for of such is the kingdom of heaven" (Matthew 19:14). Could this Jesus, who gathered little children in His arms and blessed them while here on earth, take other little children and torture them throughout eternity? Which Christ will we accept, the One who loves children or the One who tortures them? We cannot believe in both.

4. *We reject the teaching of eternal torment because the redeemed, having a part in the final judgment, could never condemn their fellow creatures—including their grandparents, parents, husbands, wives, children, and grandchildren—to unending torture.* Their sense of justice could never permit such an atrocity. "Do ye not know that the saints shall judge the world? and if the world shall be judged by you, are ye unworthy to judge the smallest matters?" (1 Corinthians 6:2).

5. *We reject the teaching of eternal torment because it imposes a punishment out of proportion to the crimes committed, thus violating the infinite justice of God.* "We are sure that the judgment of God is according to truth against them which commit such things" (Romans 2:2). "I judge: and my judgment is just" (John 5:30). "Great and marvellous are thy works, Lord God Almighty; just and true are thy ways" (Revelation 15:3).

6. We reject the teaching of eternal torment because it would forever cast a shadow over the happiness of the redeemed. Eternal life for the redeemed would be anguish beyond words when they realized that somewhere in the universe their own relatives—their flesh and blood—were being tortured, tormented, and toasted over undying flames. "God shall wipe away all tears from their eyes" (Revelation 7:17; 21:4).

7. We reject the teaching of eternal torment because it vilifies God's character and turns Him into a monstrous agent of Satan—a miracle worker who keeps the wicked alive moment by moment in a fire that burns but cannot consume, that hurts but cannot destroy. God would have to miraculously sustain the lives of those immersed in an aimless and endless punishment. Hence God would in reality become worse than Satan himself.

8. We reject the teaching of eternal torment because of the fruit its teaching has brought forth here on earth. It has caused untold thousands to turn their backs on God and become His bitterest opponents. Moreover, it has caused thousands of others to do unspeakable things to their fellowmen in the name of God with the intent of saving them from hellfire.

The medieval, Spanish, and Roman inquisitions left a trail of blood, torture, and death behind them that continues to embarrass the Roman Catholic Church today. During the reign of one inquisitor (Tomás de Torquemada) more than 2,000 heretics died by burning at the stake. Not only were baptized Christians tortured and executed for heresy, but also any Jew, Muslim, or heathen who tried to lead a Christian into unbelief or heresy.

What the Bible Teaches

Thus far we have examined the parable of the rich man and Lazarus, and the expressions "eternal fire," "everlasting fire," and smoke that ascends "for ever and ever." We have discovered that every one of these expressions—as understood by the listeners and readers of Christ's time—meant nothing more than a complete, total annihilation of the wicked.

In fact, in all the passages that people use to teach an eternally burning hellfire we have discovered, on closer examination, nothing which supports the belief that God sustains the life of the unredeemed in the lake of fire.

Eternal life is life eternal, eternal death is death eternal, and everlasting destruction is destruction with no remedy, no cure, total consumption. Only such conclusions harmonize with the justice of God and with the total picture presented by the Bible on the subject of hellfire.

The time has come to present the forthright Bible teaching on this serious subject.

The full biblical picture portrays the complete and total annihilation of the wicked in the lake of fire on the surface of planet Earth following the day of judgment (see 2 Peter 3:7, 10-12; Revelation 20:9). In more than fifty different Bible passages does God proclaim this fact most emphatically:

1. They shall die. "The soul that sinneth, it shall die" (Ezekiel 18:4; see also Ezekiel 18:26; John 8:21; Romans 6:23; 8:13; James 1:15; Revelation 21:8). Dictionaries remind us that to die means "to cease to live," "to perish," "to expire," "to cease to exist," "to become dead." To claim that death for the wicked really means some form of eternal life is no different than calling darkness light, black white, or night day.

2. They shall perish. "God so loved the world, that he gave his only begotten Son, that whosoever believeth in him should not perish, but have everlasting life" (John 3:16; see also Psalms 37:20; 92:9; John 10:28; Romans 2:12). To perish, according to the dictionaries, is "to die," "to be destroyed," "to pass away," "to waste away," "to come to nothing."

3. They shall be rooted out. "The wicked shall be cut off from the earth, and the transgressors shall be rooted out of it" (Proverbs 2:22; see also Isaiah 5:24; Malachi 4:1). Rooting out means "to pull, tear, or dig up by the roots," thereby killing the plant, "to eradicate completely."

4. They shall be slain. "With the breath of his lips shall he slay the wicked" (Isaiah 11:4). "Those mine enemies, which would not that I should reign over them, bring hither, and slay them before me" (Luke 19:27; see also Psalms 34:21; 139:19). To slay means "to kill violently, wantonly, or in great numbers," "to destroy."

5. They shall be destroyed. "The Lord preserveth all them that love him: but all the wicked will he destroy" (Psalm 145:20; see also Isaiah 13:9-11; Matthew 10:28; Revelation 11:18).

6. They shall be devoured. "What do ye imagine against the Lord? he will make an utter end: affliction shall not rise up the second time. For . . . they shall be devoured as stubble fully dry" (Nahum 1:9, 10; see also Isaiah 33:14; Hebrews 10:27; Revelation 20:7-9).

7. They shall be burned up. "The Lord reigneth; let the earth rejoice. . . . A fire goeth before him, and burneth up his enemies round about" (Psalm 97:1-3; see also Matthew 3:10, 12; 2 Peter 3:7, 10-12). The laws of physics affirm that fire cannot burn unless it has something to burn. For combustion to take place, something must be consumed, eaten, or devoured. Even atomic energy, which operates in a different manner from combustion, requires matter which can be converted into energy. Thus, the fire that devours, consumes, and burns the wicked will not keep burning after the wicked are consumed.

8. *They shall melt away.* "As wax melteth before the fire, so let the wicked perish at the presence of God" (Psalm 68:2; see also Psalm 112:10; Micah 1:4; 2 Peter 3:7, 10-12).

9. *They shall be turned into smoke.* "The wicked shall perish, and the enemies of the Lord shall be as the fat of lambs: they shall consume; into smoke shall they consume away" (Psalm 37:20; see also Psalm 68:2).

10. *They shall become ashes.* "Behold, the day cometh, that shall burn as an oven; and all the proud, yea, and all that do wickedly, shall be stubble: and the day that cometh shall burn them up, saith the Lord of hosts. . . . Ye shall tread down the wicked; for they shall be ashes under the soles of your feet in the day that I shall do this" (Malachi 4:1-3; see also 2 Peter 2:6).

A Complete Destruction

Not only shall the wicked "burn" (Greek *Kaio*—Luke 3:17), but they shall "burn up" (a much stronger Greek word, *katakaio*—Matthew 3:12). They will not only "consume," but they will "consume away" (Psalm 37:20); not only "perish," but they shall "utterly perish" (2 Peter 2:12); and not merely "eaten," but "eaten up" and "devoured" (Isaiah 51:8; Revelation 20:9). How could God possibly describe the total annihilation of the wicked more emphatically and strongly than He has in these fifty Bible passages?

From these texts we can draw only one conclusion: "The wages of sin *is* death" (Romans 6:23). The wicked do not live forever. "The soul that sinneth, it shall die" (Ezekiel 18:4). No murderer, no sinner, "hath eternal life abiding in him" (1 John 3:15). God alone possesses immortality (see 1 Timothy 1:17; 6:16; 1 Corinthians 15:53, 54). And only those who have the Son have life: "He that hath not the Son of God hath not life" (1 John 5:12).

Only two groups of people exist at the end of time—the saved and the lost (see Matthew 25:31-41). The righteous live, and the wicked die. Life and death—each is as everlasting as the other. The death of the wicked will last as eternally as the life of the righteous. Neither has an end.

A New Heaven and New Earth

How does God accomplish this annihilation of the wicked? Revelation 20 gives us a description of the sad, final events:

> When the thousand years are expired, Satan shall . . . go out . . . to gather them [the wicked] together to battle: the number of whom is as the sand of the sea. And they went up on the breadth of the earth, and compassed the camp of the saints about, and the beloved city: and fire came down from God out of heaven, and devoured them (verses 7-9).

Satan, his evil angels, and all the wicked from all ages (which have been raised in the second resurrection, called "the resurrection of damnation"—John 5:28, 29) surround the holy city of God, which has just descended out of heaven (see Revelation 21:10).

As they begin to attack the New Jerusalem—attempting to gain by sheer numbers what they couldn't conquer through deceit or treachery—God halts them in their tracks by opening the awesome books of judgment:

> I saw a great white throne, and him that sat on
> it, from whose face the earth and the heaven
> fled away; and there was found no place for
> them. And I saw the dead, small and great,
> stand before God; and the books were opened:
> and another book was opened, which is the book
> of life: and the dead were judged out of those
> things which were written in the books, accord-
> ing to their words. . . . And whosoever was not
> found written in the book of life was cast into
> the lake of fire (Revelation 20:11-15).

Following the pronouncement of God's sentence
upon the wicked, an intense fire sweeps over the face
of the earth and destroys the wicked and their works.

> The heavens and the earth, which are now, by
> the same word are kept in store, reserved unto
> fire against the day of judgment and perdition
> of ungodly men. . . . The day of the Lord will
> come as a thief in the night; in the which the
> heavens shall pass away with a great noise, and
> the elements shall melt with fervent heat, the
> earth also and the works that are therein shall
> be burned up (2 Peter 3:7-10).

This fire will forever eradicate all trace of sin and sinners. It will completely burn up the wicked and reduce
them to ashes. It will "devour" Satan, the arch-enemy
who started the whole rebellion, and reduce him to
ashes so that "never shalt [he] be any more" (Ezekiel
28:18, 19; see also Revelation 11:18). When God
destroys all wickedness, He destroys it forever: "He will
make an utter end: affliction shall not rise up the
second time" (Nahum 1:9). Sin and sinners simply will

never again exist. "Let the sinners be consumed out of the earth, and let the wicked be no more" (Psalm 104:35).

But thanks be to God, He plans something better with which to replace our old world. Following his description of the lake of fire that consumes everything, Peter declares: "Nevertheless we, according to his promise, look for new heavens and a new earth, wherein dwelleth righteousness" (2 Peter 3:13). Then will come to pass Christ's promise to His followers that "the meek . . . shall inherit the earth" (Matthew 5:5).

This earth made new will be our eternal home:

> I heard a great voice out of heaven saying, Behold, the tabernacle of God is with men, and he will dwell with them, and they shall be his people, and God himself shall be with them, and be their God. And God shall wipe away all tears from their eyes; and there shall be no more death, neither sorrow, nor crying, neither shall there be any more pain: for the former things are passed away. And he that sat upon the throne said, Behold, I make all things new. And he said unto me, Write: for these words are true and faithful (Revelation 21:3-5).

How marvelous are God's ways. His solution for the problem of sin far exceeds man's inventions and fables. And His invitation to join Him in love, joy, and service is wide open to everyone. Isn't it a joy to serve such a God and to look for His soon return? For this great event we pray, "Even so, come, Lord Jesus. Amen."

Each book in the Discovery series is a Bible study on a particular topic. Below is a partial list of topics.

Inspiration of the Bible
Where we got the Bible
How to study the Bible
The Trinity
God the Father
Jesus Christ, the Son of God
Who is the Holy Spirit?
Creation and evolution
Justification by faith
Victory over sin
The new birth
Jesus our Mediator
What happens when you die?
The Sabbath
Where Sunday came from
How to live healthfully
Marriage

Law and grace
The moral and ceremonial laws
Spiritual gifts
The gift of prophecy today
Must I belong to a church?
Baptism and communion
Rise of the antichrist
God's final judgment
The origin of evil
The mark of the beast
The Battle of Armageddon
Christ's second coming
The rapture
The millennium
Hell
Speaking in tongues
Should Christians be different?

For more information about Discovery books, write to:

Discovery Books
PO Box 5353
Nampa, ID 83653-5353

ISBN 0-8163-0756-3

9 780816 307562